THE FOREST WITHIN

THE FOREST WITHIN

SUE SUSMAN

gatekeeper press

Columbus, Ohio

The Forest Within

Published by Gatekeeper Press
3971 Hoover Rd. Suite 77
Columbus, OH 43123-2839
www.GatekeeperPress.com

Library of Congress Control Number: 2017964201

ISBN: 9781619848603
eISBN: 9781619848597

Cover photo by Sue Susman

Printed in the United States of America

For my parents who saved my life
and made everything possible.

"There is pleasure in the pathless woods."
—Lord Byron

"Not all who wander are lost."
—J.R.R. Tolkien

Contents

Even in the Dark

The forest breathes in and out
as I sleep and curl
like a cat snuggled into a bigger sleeping body.
Even in the dark,
I wake
and see light from above,
the moon burning into black earth.
Stars,
glittering chips of glass,
scatter in a strange design.
I keep my eyes open until morning.

Love Poem

Dear Sue,

This is God.

I love you more than you could ever know.
I always have
and I always will.
You are my precious child.
I was there before you were conceived
and later while your mother carried you,
holding you,
loving you
as I have all along.
And when you were born,
I held your mother in my heart,
the truth of her life passing on to you.
I filled you with it—
all the love she gave you
in the beginning.
It is what helped you grow and explore,
learn and become.
It is what you had
when you needed more than you had,
more than you thought you had.
Her love,
passed down from me,
saved you,
kept you alive,

2

helped you to uncover your true self—
pure,
whole,
as I created you.
I am always here—your Eternal Mother—
and I am always in you.

Rise Up Together and Dance

Once again I am walking,
dying,
traveling on this lonely road.
Only the sound of my heart tells me
that I am still here.
Abandoning myself
to the strange, mournful songs of night,
I begin to retrieve scattered pieces of dreams.
I am powerless to discover beauty unless I am silent,
yet silence sings to me now
of loss
and blood grown cold.
I am silent and mournful.
I abandon myself.

In the evening,
I will return to the woods
where I first learned my name,
where the tall trees
surrounded and held me.
Once again, I will wait for you.
You remind me to search for myself
with an urgency I missed in the beginning.
You stand with arms outstretched,
high above your head.
You give thanks.
You give up.
I imagine you are making the rain come.

You reach up to touch the sun,
and the moon kisses your eyes with her lips.

It is here I remember my grandmother's prayer
as she drifted in and out,
that we would all be together again
as we were in the beginning,
that the dead and the living would rise up together,
that the dead and the living
within us
would rise up together and dance.

Naked Sky

I know a place where the river runs fast and clear
and the sky gives the sunlight back to the morning.
She wants to keep it for herself,
but she thinks it should be shared.

You and I—
we run together,
snow melting off the mountain into lines of blue water,
becoming liquid sky.
Two rivers from the same source—
subterranean well,
tangible light.
Separate and whole,
we run together—
merge,
come apart
again
and I,
I split open,
and all my seeds
in neatly ordered rows
hang exposed,
stripped bare by the light in your hand.

I want to crawl back into the dark,
back inside the cave of your body.
Let me burrow deep into your darkness,
into the safety of your night.
I want to return to the place far away inside you,

where the river runs clear
and the light comes back to kiss earth in the morning.

Touch me again now.
I want to be water,
blue with light from the naked sky.

My Pleasure, My Pain

I will not apologize for wanting you—
the long, slow, lumbering
length of your body,
the low notes deep
in your throat.
Or for the joy I felt
when you looked at me that way
whenever you heard me speak,
and the way you smiled
and smiled
when I pulled your scarf,
and you—
closer,
closer still.

I will not apologize
for longing to go inside,
to know you,
to let the days run on
without counting,
let them run through our fingers
like sand.

I will not apologize
for the music in my head,
for the sound of voices singing—
your voice,
mine,
but it is only a dream.

Find Me

I am waiting for you to find me—
open me.
I am waiting to let you in.
There is nothing to stop us from loving—
nothing to get in our way.
Only warm light inside
that fills us with life.

At the Mexican Restaurant

I watch your hands cradle the white china cup,
forming a circle as you lift it up to drink.
The cup in the center seems tiny
like a little girl's tea-time plaything—
pink, delicate,
protected by these wide-open hands.

Drinking your coffee in silence,
you move water glasses on the dark-green tablecloth,
arranging them in a small triangle,
asking the waiter to fill them for me.
I say, "Spicy food makes me thirsty."
We go on.

Across this table,
words float away
like passengers on old wooden ships,
happy to finally be lost at sea.
I can hear the yellowed sails flapping in the salty air
like wings.

Inside,
something opens.
A little girl is playing tea party.
I wait to feel the kindness of your hands.

Love Song from Mother Earth

In the morning,
I will come to you
singing.
My voice will be the only sound you will hear.
But unlike the sirens' song,
I will not lure you to your death.
You will feel the wind on your body
and a soft rain will cover you.
The night you find yourself in
will set you free.

The Hot Days of Summer

At night,
stars sprinkle the darkness
and the moon with the sky in her arms
smiles gently and glows.
Everything around her is light.

Below all is green and silent.
Only the sound of crickets singing the night to sleep.

And we dream that a dragon stands at the window
    looking in,
breathing in darkness,
breathing out fire.
Even the wind feels like fire,
breathing the dragon's breath.

And the moon holds the sky in her arms
and glows.

What I Need

A tree grows forever
reaching its branches up to the sky,
but we are only human
and forever is too long to imagine.
I want to walk with you in the early morning,
through a field of sun-bleached grass
growing free,
blowing wild,
like hair suddenly unclasped in a midsummer wind.
You will not speak to me with words,
but with your eyes.
With your eyes,
dark with feeling,
fierce and loving,
you will hold me.
You will take me in,
as you have welcomed me before.
And as before,
you will rock me in the warm cradle of your heart
and soothe me.
You will give me strength.
I will gather together the scattered pieces of myself.
It will be enough of what I need.
It will be exactly what I need.

Heat

Steam rises with words
as I carry the spoon to my mouth,
burning my tongue.
I am listening to myself talking to you—
silent on the other side.
I am saying things like,
"Careful, the soup is hot."
and "I am so hungry."
Do you feel it too?
My words feel so far away.
I have lost them.
You go on watching me eat,
your eyes never leaving my face.
I grow flushed with the heat.

This is a game we are playing,
like children—
each one waiting for the other to give up.
I am playing with words here on the surface,
but each time I look up,
I dive deeper behind your eyes.
I would stay there gladly.
I would leave this place with you now,
but I need to hear words,
not promises—
words—
to draw out
the images you keep in your head.
I cannot see.
Show me.

I remember dancing,
both of us leading,
the music too loud,
the songs too short,
turning us around and around.
And in the morning,
I felt you crying silently beside me—
your breath coming too fast
like you had something caught in your throat.
It was as if the sun had gutted out a space for you,
but you hadn't learned to live there.

My words fall like small stones
in patterns around my feet.
I will have to walk over them again when I leave you.

Only Clear Space Inside

Take off the old wood and burn it.
I am leaving this part of me here.
And as I light the match to start this fire,
I feel the flames begin to jump out of me.
I am burning myself up from the inside,
and this fire burns clean,
leaves no ashes—
only clear space inside.
Now the wind picks up.
The flames grow higher.
There is no pain.

The Deep Breath of You

All I wanted was Wednesday—
just to be with you again.
I drove fast,
heart racing,
the snow gone black with dirt,
windows shut against the cold,
the gray sky.

All I wanted was you,
the deep breath of you.
I couldn't stop wanting.

When I arrived,
you came to the door,
a smile opening your face,
your arms stretched wide,
waiting to fold me in.
And I went to you
and held you
with the all the hope
in my body,
your small self
warm in my arms,
like a prayer
that keeps repeating,
saying,
"Thank you.
I am alive now.
Thank you for my life."

Moving into an Empty Space

Tonight I stood watching the stars
twinkling through the bare branches.
The air is cold
and I am alone,
here in this quiet, faraway place.
I am at peace with myself,
still somewhat afraid.
I stood,
watching the night sky,
as if it would change,
as if the tiny, white lights would move
or rearrange themselves—
the better to please my eye.
But there was no change.
The night was fixed, immutable and cold.
I am a shifting star,
fallen down from the vast, empty blackness
to burn here on the earth.
I look up to see where I came from
and the lights return my gaze.
There is no message,
no sound,
just the silent reflection of my own face
shining in the dark to remind me
that I have always been here.

The Peace Unseen

The sun rises like a lover,
pulling the covers off the sleeping city—
naked in her bed.
I seek the peace of dreams,
like a shawl to wrap myself in.
A way out,
a way in,
something better—
unseen,
but always present,
like a shawl wrapped loose around my shoulders
to cover me as I walk on.

Because there is no protection,
the wind will burn
and the rain will cut,
and the sun,
ever the jealous lover,
will chase his rivals and grow dark with rage.

Only the quiet voice—
the peace of dreams that lives within,
can cover me,
sing to me
the lullaby of life—
the peace unseen
but always there.

Grief

Oh, weave me into a whole piece.
Pull the threads tight so I do not come apart.
I need to come together now,
need to be whole
in myself—in my body.
I'm loosening my hold on the past
that is falling away from me so quickly,
falling free—leaving me alone
here in the present.
Like a hitchhiker suddenly put out
by the side of the road,
I watch my life moving away from me,
speeding into the distance
until it becomes a dot on the horizon
and disappears from view.
I stand,
watching,
waiting for the car to return,
all the time knowing that it is gone for good.
And I cry out my rage,
turning my face to the sky,
with no one but myself to blame.
I see my life stretching out before me—
a long empty road,
a country highway—
and I am standing next to it
in a muddy, overgrown ditch.
I want to bury myself in the dirty grass.
I want to hide my shame in the ground.

I beg for the earth to open up and take me in,
but there is no answer—
just the unrelenting beat of my heart
so far away I don't recognize it.
It beats louder and louder in my ears until I scream—
just to put something into the emptiness.
The silence overwhelms me.
The silence screams inside me
and I scream back because I have to answer.
But there is nothing for me to say.
No words,
only sounds come out of me now—
choked and bleating,
like an animal,
newborn and abandoned.
I curl myself into a ball in the ditch
and hug the earth,
beating my rage into the dirt,
watering the dead grass with my tears.
I wait for night to fall.
I have nothing else to cover me,
and I am so exposed
here in the chilly,
open air.

Begging the Night

She approached me in the supermarket's parking lot—
a tired-looking woman with a worn-out face,
asking if I had any change.
As I shook my head,
I felt the dimes and nickels burrow deeper
in my pocket,
my back stiffen,
my hands curl into fists.
I couldn't look her in the face
and so I hurried on,
shaking my head to lose the fear
that one day,
some day,
I could be talking to strangers in parking lots,
alone in the street,
unknown and unseen,
begging the night for change.

Vacation

Last night,
I made us chili for dinner.
I thought it was too spicy,
but you said, "No."
You liked it that way.
We talked about our day
and what we would do tomorrow.
We went to bed early
and fell asleep right away.

In my dream,
you left me.
I was so bereft,
I couldn't even cry.
In the morning,
you were still there,
your breathing slow and steady,
lost in the covers.
But I could see you.
I could feel you.
Like the truth,
you never go away.

Loving the Unknown

Now, I am here—
alone in this moment.
This time I have arrived
and the landing was good.
Open now to all meaning,
all music and darkness,
I am whole
and awake,
looking into myself,
opening to what I cannot see.

Out of Ironwood

I have been pregnant for years,
always knowing
that when my time came,
I would germinate,
so that this stalk might bear fruit.
Now there's a gaping hole in my guts,
and every time I move,
little parts fall out of me—
little pieces of empty earth
falling back to the ground that I will walk on,
feeling no pain at the loss.
I'm waiting for sprouts
to break through the brittle surface,
trying to explain the remaining parts,
that resist definition.
I'm struggling to carve myself out of ironwood,
but reluctant to take on a lasting form.
I must water the roots.
It may be too late in the season for fruit,
but I think of the roots
as I dig to uncover them,
to nurture myself
at the source.

What Love Is

Sunday afternoon in the kitchen with you,
my love.
I give you pink gladiolas—the buds full,
opening halfway up the long stem.
You lean your tall self against the sink,
listening
as I tell you how I cried because you are leaving.

Later,
something inside me opened,
let go,
resolved to help you leave—
your need to go tangible,
whole
like water rushing into an ocean—
clear,
strong,
ready to be unbound.

There is a little light in your face,
like an angel in distress,
caught up in the web of your life,
one foot out the door,
the rest of you still tied and hanging.

When will you learn
that wings were made for flying higher than this?
You must have known you would get burned,
flying so close to Earth,

dipping low to touch and taste,
bringing the kindness of your real home—
the place you left so long ago
when you came down to feel what it is to be human
and ended up aching all over,
turned inside out.

Now your innocence comes back to you,
like birds returning after a long winter.
Still, your escape seems blocked—
cut off.
Wings flap—helpless as leaves—
but there is another way.
I could loosen your wings,
untie you from Heaven.
You would still be able to hear the singing,
to walk away from this moment—from everything.
You could unravel your life
and change.
I want to witness the transformation,
as you become human,
turning into a man
who is grounded forever.
It is the price you would pay
for showing me what love is.

The Bridge That Connects Us

Tell me some stories about your life
and I will tell you some, too—
the history of all the time we didn't share.
I was waiting for a day like this,
when I could feel something,
and nothing could take it away.

On Fire

Electric and full-blown in the early air,
I ride,
a burning wire—overcharged.
I am on fire.
Alive with this pain you gave me,
I carry my bloody heart.
You have hurt me for too long.
Murdering me over and over,
year after year,
you devoured me,
and I called it love
and hated you.
Now I rise from my ashes,
red hair flying,
clinging wildly to the matted mane—
the bare back.
I will ride you till you drop.

Saturday Night

Hot time,
this summer in the city—
in the artificial light of the street.
At night people scurry and run together in packs—
too many rats in the cage,
running toward something in the distance,
in the dark,
something hidden from sight,
something they cannot name.
They come here to hunt and groan
in hot, dark rooms filled with sweating, hungry bodies,
dancing with fever into the morning.
As the music blasts into flashing strobe lights,
the walls begin to swell and breathe.
There are bodies on the street tonight—
each with its own hidden secret.
You can choose one to take home with you.
You can go on alone.
You can help yourself.
Steal into the night.
No one can find you.
You become invisible in the dark—
invisible to others who may want to hurt you,
invisible even to yourself.

Climbing into the Light

She separates her lives,
one from the other,
both from herself.
I know because she told me.
She leaves the old one silent in its cold hole,
sleeping in the dark.
And she lets her young life lead her
far away into deep woods,
over green mountains,
into quick-flowing streams.
She lets it show her a sweetness she has never known.
And she laughs and nurtures this young life
that she bore in pain and tears.
Some days she visits the old one,
deep in the hole where she left it.
She feeds it bread and water
for she knows it must survive.
It must live on without her,
so she can remember it—
so she can keep letting go of the old pain
and learn to live without it.

This Moment

On a morning like this,
I will see what I have missed before
and my story will continue,
but it will not be me who will tell it—
someone or something bigger—
ancient,
will take me further,
and I will go
and learn,
and the story will go on,
and I will go with it.

Until the Spring Trees Come Back

The gray sky wants to darken the daylight,
pulling down the darkness
like a dirty window that is always closed.
Earth is covered with snow—
the frozen ground hard as rock.

Then Heaven opens,
and rain melts the ice
until the spring trees come back—
their fullness even richer.
Flowers are growing—
a full palette of color in light.
Even the clouds look beautiful now—
white and floating,
changing in air.

Now You Are Gone

I remember my last kiss. It was you—lying there in
the hospital bed, the light going out of your eyes
like the sun going down slowly. It was nothing like
my first kiss with you—the one that surprised me
that day we were together in the forest preserve. It
was sunny and warm. We were walking. You looked
at me shyly and took both my hands. Why does
it seem so long ago now—the green of the trees
fading into memory, the way you looked at me, the
way you looked? It lasted a long time—at least it
seemed like a long time. I want to go back there and
walk again with you—the sun bright over our heads,
our movements slow, unstudied. Now you are gone.
The call came in the middle of the night—my first
punch in the stomach—the only time I have ever felt
caught. I flew to the hospital. The whole family was
there. We surrounded you—not moving. The air was
filled with shock and grief. Your body lay before us,
but you were not there. My last kiss. A world away.

Never Alone

All the love I need has found me.
I feel it in myself
and the days go on.
Nothing has changed,
but now I can love you.
Before there was nothing inside but despair.
Now there is an opening
and the light shines.
I walk through a forest
and someone takes my hand.

Father's Day

There's something in the water
that sounds like my father's breathing,
deep and husky,
makes me want to listen hard
for fear the sound might stop
and I'd be abandoned all over again.

Away off down the beach,
giggling children crawl next to each other
in the sand,
racing toward something that wants to get away.
Behind them,
a little girl runs screaming
into the waves.
I wait for her to throw her body in,
but she just sits down in the white sand
and lets the water cover her legs.

I am looking for my father,
alone on this crowded beach.
He is not here,
but I feel him all around me,
remember his heavy heart
and the sound of his voice laden with sadness
and disappointed anger.

At night he beat the air
with words curled into fists,
yearning out loud

for something he could never really name.
Frightened by the sound of him,
I huddled into my little body,
rolled my voice into a ball in my chest.

I didn't want to listen to the pain pouring out of him
or the gnawing hunger in my own heart
and so I grew up hating him,
afraid to let him see
how much I needed him to know me,
always longing to somehow be let in.

But the words were too hard between us,
and the anger hangs thick and unresolved.
Now I'm looking for my father,
though I know he isn't here.
My heart is heavy with what he gave me.
I want to pour it into the water
and let the waves wash all the heaviness away,
but the waves keep coming back
and the children are bringing tiny fish
to their smiling father,
while I carry my heavy heart.

Here I Am

I am waiting for the moment—
for all the moments,
for the time when I can open myself
to the life that is in me,
the life I have carried
all the way here.

The Star Path

The river flows in moonlight.
Stars glitter in a footpath—
Gretel's breadcrumb path through the woods—
green woods,
wild flowers,
a holy morning light.

And the river goes on
without me.
There is nothing I can do to stop or slow it down.
It doesn't know I am here
and I turn back to the path,
stars in the sky,
breadcrumbs dropped to form a memory,
a memory eaten by wild birds,
but etched in the mind,
in the night sky.

Walking,
I am walking,
and the ground kisses my feet as they fall.
I am not lost.
I am never lost.
My feet have found their own way.

The Fountain

The lights are on
in the fountain tonight,
changing colors,
turning the hissing streams pink.
We stand here in darkness.
I have never seen you cry.
The tears,
so sudden,
surprise you
like a lover coming back
or leaving.
You shake your head for clarity,
for me to tell you the pain is false,
as if part of your body were missing,
taken from you—
cold and aching for completeness.
I know this feeling.
Strange that we should only share an empty space.
We try to soothe ourselves,
and you—always stoic,
neither revealing or searching emotion—
now bury your face in my shoulder.
What can I do but hold you?
The wall is still intact,
and I will always care.

Leaning into the Wind

Don't you see?
There is nothing you can do
to stop or slow me down.
I am moving ahead to a place I've never been.
Try to follow if you can,
but I will not wait for you.
I am going alone
and I am not afraid.

Everything That's Living

My body knows this road,
the unforgiving blacktop,
the soft, gentle slope,
the long way home.
I am coming out of winter,
snow and ice still melting,
driving fast—
bearing down on this long, empty highway.
Like a skin pulled taut,
it seems to have no end,
and I go on,
moving forward
in this cool, bright morning,
part of everything that's living,
here in this whole, connected world.

The Night Tree

In the distance,
in the dark,
I talk hard to an old tree.
Winding round and round,
I am a flame
and the tree welcomes me.
I don't need a reason to be here.
There is time enough to understand.
My name is the sound of the wind blowing
and my spirit is old.
Until the sky grows light,
I will stay here
and listen to the way the dark feels.
The fire in my throat burns more quietly now.
I can hear the empty sound of dawn.

Scatter My Ashes

Scatter my ashes before I die.
Let me blow and fade in the wind,
over water,
into nothing.
Watch me dissolve in air.
Scatter my old bones.
I am keeping the young ones—
fresh, strong—the blood circles
and weaves me into a whole piece
with long, slender red thread
buried under my skin.

The Fire Tender

I remember the darkness and me alone in it,
burning the fire in the blackness of earth
and no water to put out the pain—
only wind
that fanned the flames higher,
hotter,
until I made magic in the black night,
danced wild-eyed under trees,
desperate in the dark.
No moon—only white specks for stars.
I couldn't even see myself—
transparent and fading in the cold black air.
I made medicine to make myself live.
I taught myself how to forgive,
and I forgave.
I forgave myself.
I am still dancing,
now smiling,
burning into the dark,
circling the fire inside,
letting the smoke rise.
We have burned before for less.

This Way Is Better

I tear myself away too soon.
Pulling off the safety belt,
I jump from a moving car.
Too late to get back in.
The ride has ended
and the car speeds away.
I have overstayed the time here
and now I must walk on.
Scraped hands and knees—
no matter.
I will heal them with work and careful attention,
always praising the advantage of time.

The Healing Trees

In the early light,
I walked into the forest,
craving her darkness,
losing myself in the green of trees,
begging my feet to carry me
and the earth to take me in.
"Come," she beckoned—
in the wind,
in the laughing leaves,
and I walked and walked until I grew tired,
until I sat down,
leaning up against a thick, old tree,
searching the early sky.

I wish I could go back—go home,
but I'm stuck in glass and concrete,
in this box here in the sky.
I put the phone down,
shaking,
wondering where to put this scream inside me.
Next to it there is a crack,
opening wider—deeper.
I want to jump in.
Words are all I have,
so I call a different number.
Desperate...I lay out my bloody heart
and pray for anything to hold me.

Across this distance,
your words become thread,
sewing me back together.
Words fill this space
growing large,
gaping—
empty.
Your voice echoes,
calling me from a distant mountain—
words falling like soft rain.
I open to the sound.
Lost on a rocky, winding path,
I stumble in the dark.
Now your voice begins
in a canyon far beyond these mountains,
reaches me—
finally,
whispers in my ear,
"Love yourself, sister.
Live."

Return Me to Me

I want my body back.
Give it to me.
It's mine.
I wasn't looking when you slipped it out from under,
quiet as a ghost.

Now I am a ghost,
move silently in and out of corners,
hang from ceilings,
crouch behind doors.
You can't see me,
but you know I'm there.

I'm as cool and clear as deadly vapors,
and I float in your direction.
You can't see me,
but you know I'm there.

I'm as quiet as a rape on the other side of town.
The woman died,
but you didn't hear her scream.

I am the thorn
that you drove through your tender, naked foot
when you stepped on the blood-red rose.

The Cool Shelter of Earth

The moon slides down behind the yellow sun,
disappears each day at the purple dawn,
but my shame glitters,
calls out loud in this light.
I dig a hole,
big enough for all of me,
and climb down into the cool shelter of earth.
Turning in this darkness,
I open slowly like a bright flower,
singing color into night.

Eternal Light

Heart in the darkness,
holding onto the light inside.
Inside, there is a spark—
a light that burns
and never goes out,
never grows dim,
but burns hard and bright
in the dark void of unending night,
the vast, empty blackness of my self
where I can only hear the echo of my cavernous soul
and the simple cadence of my healthy heart,
hurting and healing over and over,
pumping life into my veins,
pushing it around and through,
so that I am always filled with it,
so that I am always alive to the light—
even when I am lost and wandering,
lonely in the dark.

An Old, Old Woman...

crackles like a gramophone disc—
the tune still audible though the words are fading.
She smiles with watery eyes
at unfamiliar faces,
family members
whose names she has forgotten.
The visits are so few.
Despite contented rocking,
that hideous clamor will not be calm.
It speaks with her when she talks,
describing memories.
The past will not die for her,
but continues to the present.
The grooves deepen with each turn.
The needle point grows dull,
but sound keeps coming forward.
She gives advice.
The story unwinds.
Old friends—now dead,
still talk to her sometimes.
She remembers back to a time before the circle broke
and she went pacing wearily
to catch the straying end.

Leaves of Light

There's a tree in my heart.
It has been there for so many years,
waiting for me to find it so I can crawl in,
climb up into her branches and sigh.
I will sing when I find you.
I will scatter the earth of your soul
with red rose petals I bring you
from the world outside.

My Grandmother Leaving

I learned of your death from a message someone left
on my answering machine.
They told me what time you had died—
as if that made a difference,
as if time could bring you back
or fill the hole in me.
For days, I hardly spoke,
had no words,
pulled the covers over my head,
tried to turn the world off.
Somewhere, I heard a door closing
and footsteps leading away,
down a long hall.
I saw myself leaving your house
for the last time,
leaving you over and over
like a rewinding movie—
leaving you inside.
You couldn't come with me,
so you just stayed behind.

In the Kitchen, Talking

The newspaper cracked the air like thunder,
pushed me farther back in my chair,
the breakfast table stacked with dishes
and unfinished sentences,
waiting.
I sat alone with my father,
listening to his breathing,
watching him turn the pages,
longing to be let in,
to be read and opened—
to be studied like these pages
every morning
before he puts on his jacket
and walks out the door,
on his way to work.

I have news.
All my catastrophes are gone now and fading.
And from this distance,
this memory of distance,
I call.
Your voice softens.
I can hear your whole body pay attention.
These words—my stories,
are all you want to know.

Standing in the kitchen,
I don't know where I am.
I'm not sure who you are.

The man with the newspaper
has grown older,
like me—
has softened,
like I have,
wants to know me,
wants to love me,
wants me to let him in.

It's so fragile—
this flimsy wall between us.
I feel it flutter
like tissue
or the wings of a moth that flies to fire
and doesn't fly way.
But time is running out.
If I burn again,
I'll heal.
If I leave,
I'll miss my father—
this man I want to know,
this part of me I fear and cherish,
this life that gave me life.

Earth Music

The Earth has opened its arms to me.
I walk in,
singing.
I walk in.
Alive to the light inside me,
alive to the light and music I feel around me.
There is no end to this life I am finding—
only a new beginning
that keeps happening every day.

What Holds Us Up

Today,
a tree has fallen,
silent in the arms
of loving companions—
those left behind,
faces turned upward,
arms still open,
bereft,
still standing,
still.

Inconsolable this morning—
the one who remembers the long way back
together,
whose presence was constant
then,
now,
is here for the afterward,
held up
in the arms of loving companions.
Still.

And now there is no answer.
Faces turned upward seek refuge.
Tears do not stop.
Prayers, spoken and not,
family connected by blood
and by love.
All who loved

and love.
All who hold us up—
we hold,
still.

This New Life

Alone,
I remember
how many times I hugged you,
knowing I would see you again—
my friend.

Now when I put my arms around you,
I have to let go.
The light in your eyes,
even illness can't take.

What is love,
now that you are going far away?
I see you moving
down a long, open road,
a way I cannot follow.
The smile never leaves your face
as you go on—
fearless now,
safe,
all the time longing
to begin this new life you will be living
in a place we cannot go.

Full with Fire

There is so much inside me
that wants to come out,
that needs to come forward
and be seen,
heard,
opened
like a letter
or a box wrapped in ribbons,
under a tree.

This Winter Light

So cold,
this winter light.
Even the sky is white,
like breath exhaled,
the sleeping breath of a whole city,
turning into steam in the frozen air,
becoming this white blanket that covers the ground.

Earth will rest underneath,
covered like a sleeping child.
And in the spring,
when the ice flows,
she will awaken,
turning,
always turning
into something better,
into something new.

Let my prayer for love be a lullaby
that comforts more than me.
Make my song as hopeful as birds that sing,
even now,
when there is so little light.

Blue Light

The world has opened its arms to me.
I walk in,
singing.
Nothing will stop me now.
There is nothing I am afraid of—
only love
in me
and around me.
I too,
am open,
and life fills me.
I am flying.
I touch the sky
and get lost in an ocean
of blue light.

As I Open My Heart

In the morning,
I will find you.
I will come to you,
singing,
with all my heart open
and my body alive with light and longing.
I will gather you up—
your glorious self,
and hold you.

I will love you
until there is nothing more to give,
but there will always be more.
There is an endless supply of love
from the earth beneath us
and our Mother inside.

The Traveler

You travel my country.
You shelter my heart.
You follow the sound of the singing inside.
There is much ground to cover—
a long way to go.
But you go on—
alive to the light,
the color and music I've carried so long.

When I felt you beside me,
I unlocked the door
and you opened me.
Now you have found me—
a long-distance traveler
from a faraway place.
I will open my heart,
let you travel my country.
You can teach me your own songs
and then let me in.

Tonight there is no moon
and all the stars have gone away.
But I know you are here.
I feel your soft breath on my skin.
I wait for your touch
and for you to let me in.
Let me travel your country
and listen to your heart.
I can hear it all night,
calling my name.

Invisible Steps

I was drawn to your light.
Now I have my own light,
but I can still hear the music
and the singing inside you.
The sound draws me closer.
All I can do is dance.

Against an Autumn Sky

The leaves are returning to earth now—
little pieces of red and yellow
like tiny sails floating in air.
The tree stands still,
fixed in its place,
wind blowing harder.
The leaves fall fast,
sails puffing outward.
They are dying again now,
becoming thin and brown,
coming apart as they have before,
twisting and lonely,
against an autumn sky.

Grounding

There's a whole world inside you
and I cry for it every day.
Please let me in.
I have come a great distance to find myself here.
Inside you is freedom
and the days go on.
I don't try to hide this longing
as it leads me into deep, green forests
and this full moon.
Suddenly I am lost,
but there is plenty of light.
I can feel my body breathing.
I am taking you in.

Celebration

Once upon a time,
there was darkness inside.
I couldn't find my way.
The walls closed in around me—
cold,
carved from stone.

All I could do was shudder and cry.
And as I sat,
something made me stop.
From far away,
I heard a voice singing—
a still, small voice growing louder,
sweeter,
but there was no one else around.

Then the voice went on
and I followed it into the darkness,
knowing I had to.
There was nowhere else to go.
Then another voice joined in
and I realized it was mine.
A song of two voices singing together,
until the walls fell away.

Now I find myself dancing
for the first time
in a long time—
arms outstretched,
head thrown back,
looking up to the sky.

Beauty Mark

Life stamps itself on a soul
in indelible ink—
a beauty mark growing larger with the years.
Nothing is wasted or forgotten.
And tears are like footprints
leading out of a sea of grief and pain.

The Long Walk Home

A low thunder keeps repeating in the distance,
like an old man moving slowly,
time dissolved in air.
Light shines down through budding leaves,
turning the morning sky into pale shades of green.

Here we stand without you,
your life like a poem you never stopped writing,
sweet music that continues without end.
A gentle refrain goes on and on,
bittersweet and lovely.
There is nothing we can do,
but join in the singing
and remember you together.

We watch you moving down a long, empty, open road,
arms outstretched to share the beauty left inside you,
all you can carry
on the long walk home.

Home

Coming back home to myself,
so much along the way,
a long road I thought was leading nowhere.
Now I see where I was headed all along.

90404015R00046

Made in the USA
Lexington, KY
11 June 2018